BARRON'S

1000
DOG NAMES

Names accompany us throughout life
and are part of our personalities.
The same is true for our most faithful
companion: a dog's name represents
ownership and affection, and should
reflect its character. This practical
book will help you find the right name
for your pet.

Contents

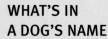

WHAT'S IN A DOG'S NAME

What's Important in a Dog's Name	5
The Mystery of the Right Name	6
Test: Your Dog's Type and Character	8
When Dog Names Are a Fashion Statement	10
Tip: A Family Conference for Naming the Dog	10
A Name Is an Invisible Leash	11
DOG TRAINING BASICS	12
The Basics of Breed Names	14
Special: Dog Horoscope	15
A NAME TRAINING PROGRAM	16

THE BEST DOG NAMES FROM A TO Z

THE BEST NAMES FOR MALE DOGS 20

Unforgettable Dogs 21

The Best Names for Pirates and Adventurers 25

The Top Ten for Male Dogs 26

The Funniest Names from Comics and Cartoons 29

THE BEST NAMES FOR FEMALE DOGS 33

Classical Names from Mythology 34

Love Comes with Spaghetti 35

The Top Ten for Female Dogs 37

The Most Outstanding Names for Smart Dogs 40

His Master's Voice 42

APPENDIX

Index 46

Addresses 47

GOOD TO KNOW AND AMUSING

You will find stories about dogs on pages 23, 28, 30, 35, 38, and 42.

What's In a
Dog's Name

A fish named Wanda? Only in the movies. Ornamental fish usually swim around without a name in an aquarium. All other pets get a name. With a dog it has to be the right one: the name should describe its character and appearance and be an expression of its personality.

What's Important in a Dog's Name

Names change the world. They give shape, make it easier to communicate and live together, and help strangers become friends. Names transmit feelings and longings, and firm up the bonds with people and other animals. House pets' names are symbolic of the trust and affection between human and animal. We unconsciously confer a different status onto an animal that we name: it changes from being a *thing* to a fellow creature and a partner. Among all the animals that humans have chosen as companions and houseguests, the dog is the one closest to us. We share our lives with dogs much more than we do with cats. They are partners in sports and games, they accompany us on trips and vacation, and they are trusted friends and comforters. The former watchdog and work animal has turned into humankind's best friend— a full-fledged family member, a chum, a protector of children, and a faithful companion for singles and seniors. A dog's name should express all that: closeness, affection, belonging, and dependability.

And yet there's much more: A name should fit its bearer naturally; it should describe the appearance and temperament, the origin, and even individual characteristics. Frequently the proud owners confer onto their four-legged partner their own expectations and demands by means of a name. And with a little puppy that will grow into a real dog, that's not always appropriate. The breeders of pedigree dogs have it easier: all dogs in a breeder's line bear the same kennel name (see page 14). A name accompanies a dog for its whole life, and it and its humans must deal with it in all situations. With cats, you can allow your fantasy free rein and give them the wildest and most adventurous names imaginable. They don't listen to them, and go their own way. People go about in public with their dogs, and the name binds them to their owners like an invisible leash and protects them and others from danger (see page 11). A dog's name must be fit for everyday duty, and every dog must learn early on to listen to its name.

The Mystery of the Right Name

A custom name. There are as many dog names as grains of sand at the beach: traditional ones, names for calling and cuddling, names of prominent animals from films, television, and literature, comical names and trendsetters, names of show champions and lifesavers, and of course, fantasy names.

Here are some things to consider in naming your dog:

➤ Your dog will learn one- or two-syllable names more quickly (see page 17).

➤ Key to praising and scolding is the tone of voice. Stretched-out vowel sounds guarantee you the dog's undivided attention.

INFO
TERMS OF ENDEARMENT ARE EFFECTIVE

➤ Pet names are an expression of our intense relationship with our dogs.

➤ The best choices for terms of endearment are short words and special names that end in i or y: *Maxi, Blacky, Fifi, Teddy,* and so forth.

➤ Combine the name with some petting as frequently as possible. That way your dog will come gladly and reliably whenever it's called.

➤ If a reprimand is necessary, don't use the pet name, but rather "Off!" or "No!"

> *Man, what a sweetheart! A cute puppy often tempts you to give it a "kid's" name. But don't forget that even the most delightful puppy will turn into an adult dog. And it should have a name that truly fits.*

TIP
THE SIZE OF THINGS

Small dogs often have strong personalities. Why not document their inner size with the name? Your Yorkshire will be well served by Minimax. Or maybe Lionheart for a feisty Jack Russell terrier . . .

➤ The name must be acceptable to the whole family and everyone who lives with the dog (see Tip, page 10).

➤ Little children often can't pronounce long, complicated names correctly. The simpler, the better.

➤ If possible, settle on a single name. If there is a shortened form or a corresponding nickname, be practical and choose the shorter one (such as Cleo from Cleopatra).

➤ A dog's name should not evoke any negative connotations. Otherwise people will easily transfer unpleasant memories of people or situations to the dog.

➤ Avoid taboo names. Dog names should neither offend religious convictions nor make fun of people.

➤ Avoid awkward and embarrassing names. It's done to be funny, but who wants to call out in the park for Piglet or Killer?

➤ Forget trendy names. The names of prominent television and movie dogs bring glamour into the house. But remember: whereas stars will be gone tomorrow, your dog will bear the name for its whole life.

➤ Consider the question of dignity. A name shouldn't demean a dog. Double-whopper and Stinky are no names for a dog.

Prince and Princess

The best food, a care-free life, exacting care, and endless dedication. Anybody who is anybody knows what it's worth. And has his own demands.

Pirate and Adventurer

Outdoors is where it's happening. Annoying the neighbor's cat, looking for a mate, nosing around in unknown places: that's life.

Macho and Maestro

Here comes the boss. Not always simple for the colleagues in the same party. But for its master and owner, it will go through any fire.

Type and Character Test

➤ A change of food turns into a family crisis.
➤ It is jealous of everything and everyone.
➤ It loves spending the twilight hour with you.
➤ It is concerned about looking well groomed.
➤ It is rather standoffish with other dogs.
Astrological sign: Pisces (See page 15.)
Name list: page 22

➤ It hits the road on its own hook.
➤ It stands longingly at the door.
➤ It's absolutely crazy about games and sports.
➤ It doesn't shy away from trouble with dogs.
➤ It's a born jogging partner.
Astrological sign: Aquarius, Sagittarius, Gemini (See page 15.)
Name list: page 25

➤ It watches reliably over house and yard.
➤ It is happy to show other dogs who's boss.
➤ It takes orders only from you.
➤ It is peerless as a protector of the children.
➤ It acts superior in every situation.
Astrological sign: Leo and Aries (See page 15.)
Name list: page 31

Baby Boomer and Mommy's Sweetheart

Gourmet treats from the hand, sleeping in bed, not having to fear nasty dogs. How nice that someone cares.

Moody and Sleeping Beauty

"Don't touch me!" is the façade. Sensitive, shy, and quick to take offense. Deep on the inside, but crazy about cuddling and loving.

Cuddlebug and Couch Potato

A walk? No, thanks. The couch is the navel of the world. And cuddling with Mistress is a real exercise in fitness— for the soul.

Where Does Your Dog Fit In?

➤ Outdoors it always stays right by you.
➤ It is the most lovable beggar of all.
➤ It runs for cover when it meets strange dogs.
➤ It becomes panic-stricken if left alone.
➤ It always wants to be hand-fed.
Astrological sign: Virgo and Capricorn (See page 15.)
Name list: page 36

➤ It always keeps its distance from strangers.
➤ It is hurt if you have no time for it.
➤ You never know exactly what it wants.
➤ It is a sweetheart when alone with you.
➤ It can go for hours without blinking.
Astrological sign: Cancer and Scorpio (See page 15.)
Name list: page 39

➤ Its daily nap times are sacred.
➤ Wants nothing more than to cuddle all day.
➤ You have to drag it out for a walk.
➤ It watches jealously over its resting spot.
➤ As a listener and soul mate it's the best.
Astrological sign: Taurus and Libra (See page 15.)
Name list: page 41

When Dog Names Are a Fashion Statement

The times are changing. So are the names.

Names are always a sign of the times, a glimpse into life and current trends. That's particularly true for dog names. Prominent four-legged examples are often the force behind their less-well-known colleagues. The comparison is simple: the more famous the dog, the greater the number of its name-sakes. It's easy to see what motivates their owners to choose the famous given names. A glimmer of the glamour for their partner and the secret hope that some of the character traits and talents of the star might slumber in the dog. When the dog is of the same breed as the star in the limelight, the master and the dog really have it made.

Many names are inextricably bound to certain breeds. It is almost an insult to swim against the current with other names. The film and TV legend Lassie (see page 24) has not only bequeathed its name to countless generations of collies, but is also the archetype of the collie. Lassie is an evergreen, like the playful St. Bernard Beethoven, or Pluto, Disney's eternal comic figure. Many other dog stars were only shooting stars, however, and have long been forgotten: who still remembers Bullet, an early star of a television series, Rocky's bullmastiff Butkus or Richard Nixon's Checkers? Who knows if the TV dog from *Frasier,* Eddie, the curly mutt Benji, or the earthy Bordeaux mastiff Hooch from *Turner and Hooch* will survive the passage of time?

Classic and Timeless

People who choose a trendy name for their dog may appear old before they wish. It's less likely to have to deal with faded celebrity when a classical name is chosen. The resonant names from world literature and mythology have their devoted circle of friends. Zeus and Hera, Romulus and

TIP
A FAMILY CONFERENCE FOR NAMING THE DOG

Single people have an advantage in choosing a name for their dog: their own favorite name always wins out. Many name givers have their own hero: Grandma dreams of the Dachshund of her youth, the kids go into raptures about some four-legged TV star, Mom insists on a kid's name, and Dad wants to calm the waters. Here's the best way to deal with that: Everyone jots down their name of choice and three other favorites. The family meets to discuss the pros and cons until only two names remain. Then it's put to a vote, and the majority wins.

Remus, and George and Lenny never make it into the top ten of favorite dog names, but they are far from second-rate.

And sometimes a traditional name gets its second wind from new cousins, such as Kevin, which has been popular ever since the hit movie *Home Alone*. Others have been a mystery for many years: you don't bump into Mr. Peabody on every street corner, even though the *Rocky and Bullwinkle Show*, in which the time-traveling dog Mr. Peabody and his boy Sherman played a major role, was enjoyed by children for years, and Steinbeck's Charley will surely survive through many generations of poodles.

A **Name** Is an Invisible Leash

In naming a cat, a parakeet, a mouse, or a hamster, you give your imagination free rein; rarely is there any practical significance connected to the names. But with dogs the right name is an invisible leash that the owner uses to lead and control the animal. To give a dog a command, you first have to get its attention. That works best with a familiar name. The best bet is a short, one- or two-syllable name that can't be confused with commonly used words. A dog named *Soot* that knows the command *Sit!* will generally put its bottom down when it hears its name. Dogs are very observant, and they react predictably to our body language and gestures. In calling a dog's name you should stand up straight and in front of the dog. When it makes eye contact, you give the desired command and use a hand signal to reinforce it (see Name Training, page 16). As with commands, go easy with the name. Anyone who yells, "Buddy, Buddy!" ten times and runs after the dog gesticulating wildly shouldn't wonder if the dog turns a deaf ear to master and mistress.

Dog Training
Basics

THE GROUND RULES FOR OBEDIENCE

Every family dog should know and obey the most important commands. That's the only way to avoid risk on a walk and around traffic, to stop undesirable behavior, and at the same time, to solidify the relationship with the four-legged partner.

Keeping it Playful with Puppies

A puppy is old enough for adoption at the age of eight to ten weeks. In the preceding time, the clumsy fellow has already learned quite a lot, especially by observing its mother's behavior, but also in dealing with its siblings. Now it's up to you to assume the role of mother and teach your new partner what's acceptable and what's not. Every dog brings along a natural readiness to learn and fit into the family pack. These tasks can be accomplished easily and playfully with a young dog. The most important lessons of basic training are intended to keep the dog under control in all situations. The dog must grow accustomed to the leash, come when called, stop on command, sit, lie down, and wait when told to do so. A dog has a short attention span: begin with short, easy exercises, give commands gently and calmly, and praise and pet the student for every successful action. You can also provide a little treat from time to time. A little play added in provides fun and strengthens motivation.

Dog training is built on trust and affection. Basic training and obedience training make sense only with a dog that accepts its master and acknowledges that person as the boss.

A dog learns particularly easily and quickly when it is motivated to cooperate and is praised generously after every successful performance. Food can be used frequently as a motivator.

A dog that has learned its lessons knows the rules—on the leash, with respect to strangers, and with other dogs. The dog always knows what's expected of it, even without express commands.

TIP
REALLY INTO LIVING

Social contacts are what really count for young dogs. Even before it's four months old a dog should get to know as many people, other dogs, and other animals as possible. Early socialization prevents possible behavior problems later on. The ideal place for stimulating encounters is puppy school.

Successful dog training is based on positive reinforcement. Every dog wants to please the leader of the pack and is proud when it does something right and receives praise. You must scold only with words ("No!" or "Out!"), never by hitting.

Experience and patience are important in correcting faulty behavior with adult dogs, especially when these behaviors have gone on for a long time. Often these dogs have to go back to basic training to repeat the missing instruction. The same is true here as with students who are initially set in their ways: petting and praise can work wonders.

The **Basics** of **Breed Names**

There are over 150 dog breeds that are officially recognized by the American Kennel Club, also known as the AKC. In order for a dog to be registered with the AKC, the registration of the litter must be completed before the registration of an individual dog from that litter. The pedigree and "personal identification" of a purebred dog is the profile that accompanies it for its entire life. In addition to the breed, sex, date of birth, color, registry number, and names of its forebears, the AKC is where the name of the dog and the name of the breeder are recorded. Dogs registered with the AKC are eligible to take part in various AKC-sponsored events, such as agility games, obedience tests and, of course, dog shows. The breeding papers and the kennel name are important for dog shows as well as if you want to breed your own dog. In real life with a dog, people use a practical given name, such as Max, instead of, for example, Maximilian of the Barren Ground.

Purebred dogs can be purchased from a breeder, but they can also be adopted from breed rescue groups. Many breeds have their own rescue group who take in and foster purebred dogs and place them in homes. Or, if you're in the market for a family pet and owning a purebred dog isn't a priority, there's always your local animal shelter.

There are many dogs in need of permanent homes who would love to go home with you. Wherever you find your beloved furry friend, make sure you choose a name that fits.

The **Right** to a Familiar **Name**

With a grown dog, you shouldn't try any experiments—you should stick to the accustomed given name. That makes it easier for the dog to adapt. Only in rare cases does a name change make sense. For example, if the dog Bruno and a grandfather named Bruno live under the same roof, or the name produces painful reactions, a change is justified. Then choose a name that's close to the old one to avoid confusing your pet.

The Stars Don't Lie

THE DOG HOROSCOPE

ARIES
March 21–April 19
Aries dogs are real characters: plucky, independent, and spirited. They need a leader to tell them what's what.

TAURUS
April 20–May 20
Unshakable, perhaps a bit phlegmatic, Taurus dogs are faithful to the end and best friends to children.

GEMINI
May 21–June 21
Charming, lively, and always ready for fun, the Geminis among dogs are no fools.

CANCER
June 22–July 22
Cancer dogs are born listeners, faithful, and affectionate, but extremely sensitive. Obedient? Sometimes.

LEO
July 23–August 22
This is the king, and it doesn't tolerate any rivals. A Leo dog is the best friend for all times.

VIRGO
August 23–September 22
Lovable, reserved, and bashful, Virgo dogs are perfect for single people, less suited to noisy children.

LIBRA
September 23–October 22
Libra dogs are sociable, outgoing, and tolerant. They prefer the comfortable life and know how to get it.

SCORPIO
October 23–November 21
Strong-willed, egocentric, thin-skinned, and quick to get into a huff. With Scorpio dogs things never get dull.

SAGITTARIUS
November 22–December 21
Physically fit to hyperactive, this dog likes turmoil and adventure. It's ready for anything and everything.

CAPRICORN
December 22–January 19
The Capricorn dog is constant and loyal; it can also be reserved. It is more of a loner than a party animal.

AQUARIUS
January 20–February 18
The Aquarius dog sometimes rides the devil. But otherwise, it is a darling—sociable and loving.

PISCES
February 19–March 20
Playful, affectionate, and good-natured, Pisces dogs come with their own positive outlook on everything.

The character types that match the horoscope are on pages 8 and 9.

A **Name**
Training Program

DOG TRAINING STARTS WITH A NAME

Your dog's name is associated with attentiveness and affection; it's used with commands, praise, and scolding. Start name training as soon as your dog comes into your home. Only when it hears its name reliably can you start basic training.

Does Your Dog **Like** Its **Name?**

We like to do only the things that are fun and useful. We ignore duties that have negative associations. So why should things be any different with dogs? They are world champions at not listening to or ignoring people if the word they are hearing

"Daisy, come!" The familiar name lets the dog know it's being spoken to and encourages it to react to your command. Playful exercises make training enjoyable for the puppy.

The sound of your voice is more important to the dog than the meaning of the command. Praise it with kind words when it listens to its name and comes to you. Your praise is an important honor for the dog.

Checklist

✔ Your dog must react enthusiastically to its name. Especially with a young dog, connect name training with praise or treats.

✔ A dog learns a short, one- or two-syllable name with particular ease.

✔ Use only one name. This applies to everyone who deals with your dog.

✔ Your dog has very fine hearing and knows from the tone of your voice what you expect from it. The word content has no meaning for the dog.

✔ Speak with a calm, subdued voice. Yelling will only frighten the dog. Scold bad behavior with harshly spoken words.

✔ Always call it by name, and never without reason.

sound scolding or angry. The name is the decisive basis for harmony and devotion. Especially in the learning phase, the dog should connect the calling of its name only with pleasant situations. As you pet it, show it a snack and call it by name once again. Connect praise with the dog's name: "Good, Morris!" or "Smart dog, Morris!" The leash is a help with dogs that are easily distracted. A gentle tug on the leash gets the dog's attention. As soon as it looks at you, tempt it with its name and a treat. If it doesn't react, repeat the exercise, but never drag it by the leash. Start name training in quiet surroundings, then try it later in situations that offer distractions.

The Best
Dog Names
from A to Z

The 1000 best dog names offer you a colorful and varied mixture of the extravagant and the noble, contemporary and traditional, exotic and clever—divided by male and female. You are guaranteed to find the perfect name for your pal.

Hello,
My Name Is . . .

The little heartbreaker needs a name. It should express character and personality, sound good, and of course be appropriate for everyday use. It's no easy task to decide on a dog name that you'll have to live with and like for many years. The 1000 best dog names in this book were determined by practicality, frequency, sound, and originality. Most names have one or two syllables; longer dog names or ones that involve several words are hardly ever used in daily practice. Even in some foreign countries there is a trend toward choosing English and American names. The reason is that the names are usually short and sound pleasing when spoken. In the supplementary lists you will find the best dog names from literature, the most cherished names for couples and partners, the most famous movie dogs, and much more. The comical and unusual stories from a dog's life guarantee your reading pleasure.

The Best Names
for Male Dogs

Ace *Batman's dog, top-notch and first-rate*

Achilles *The hero in the Trojan war in Homer's* The Iliad

Acrobat *Greek for "walking on tiptoe," good for a dog who can do tricks*

Adam *Means "from the earth," ideal for a firstborn pup*

Ad lib *For the dog that acts extemporaneously and likes to improvise*

Admiral *High ranking, deserving of respect, admirable*

Adonis *A beautiful individual, the god of beauty, youth*

Aesop *Author of fables, a wise character*

Afro *A curly, fuzzy hairstyle*

Al *Noble, illustrious, short for Albert*

Alchemist *Magician who can turn metals into gold*

Alex *Defender of mankind, Alexander the Great*

Alibi *Good for a dog that's often in trouble and needs an excuse*

Alpha *Number one dog, dominant, the TV dog on* Bewitched

Amadeus *Wolfgang Amadeus Mozart, composer of classical music*

The Best Names from World Literature

Alice: a dream trip through Wonderland; Scout: from the classic book *To Kill a Mockingbird*; Stella: a classical play by Goethe; Quixote: the Knight of the Sad Countenance; Tarzan: Edgar Rice Burroughs's King of the Jungle; Sinbad: a seaman in *The Arabian Nights*; Hamlet: Shakespeare's tragic prince of Denmark; Rochester: the emotional, tragic character from *Jane Eyre*.

Amaretto *Italian almond-flavored liqueur*

Ambros *Good name for a large, dark dog*

Amigo *Spanish for "friend"*

Amor *Roman god of love*

Andy *Short for Andrew, also André in French*

Angus *Outstanding, excellent; good for a herding dog, also Gus*

Antonio *TV dog on the* Drew Carey Show

Anubis *Egyptian god resembling a pharaoh hound*

Apache *Native American tribe, ideal for a dog with patches*

Apollo *God of prophecy, TV dog in* Magnum PI

Archie *Noble and bold*

Argent *French for "silver"*

Argo *Greek for "fast, quick," the ship Jason sailed to find the Golden Fleece*

Argos *Odysseus's loyal hunting dog in Homer's* The Odyssey *who waited 20 years for Odysseus's return*

Argyle *Tartan or pattern from a clan tartan, also Argyll*

Aries *First sign of the zodiac, for a dog with a strong personality*

Aristotle *Famous Greek philosopher*

Arlo *Singer Arlo Guthrie*

Armani *Designer, fashion label*
Ascot *Fashionable tie or scarf*
Ash *Ideal name for a gray or grayish white dog*
Aspen *Good name for a golden-colored dog*
Astro *Meaning "star," the dog on the animated cartoon series* The Jetsons
Atlas *For a strong dog; in Greek mythology, Atlas carried the world on his shoulders*
Atticus *The kind, wise lawyer in* To Kill a Mockingbird
Attila *King of the Huns*
Audacity *Courage, boldness, daring*
Augustus *Nobility, high rank, as the ruler Caesar Augustus*
Aussie *Nickname for an Australian native, ideal for an Australian breed*
Austin *Revered individual, short for Augustine*
Avalanche *Cascade of snow, good name for a white dog*
Avalon *Mythical paradise island in King Arthur's time*
Avery *Strong and powerful*
Axel *Reward, source of life*

Badger *A fearless, tenacious animal, the hero in* Wind in the Willows
Bailey *An Irish liqueur or castle casing, ideal name for a terrier or protective dog*
Baldric *Valiant and courageous, fearless prince, ruler*
Ballyhoo *Noisy uproar, loud talk*
Balto *Famous dog that delivered medical supplies in Alaska; in the animated movie about Balto, he is portrayed as half wolf, half husky*
Bambino *Italian for "baby"*
Bandit *Mischievous and into trouble*
Banjo *Good for a lively southern dog*
Banner *For a dog that excels, a good representative*
Barkly *A dog that barks a lot, also Barkley*
Baron *A rank of nobility*
Barry *From the children's book,* Barry: The Bravest Saint Bernard *by Lynn Hall*
Basil *Majestic, also Bazil*
Baxter *Short, simple, and fun name*
Beamer *Great name for a fancy dog, after the luxury car (BMW)*
Bear *A cuddly teddy-bear type or a big, strong kind of dog*
Beau (Bo) *Very handsome, dashing*

UNFORGETTABLE DOGS

Barry: the original St. Bernard, reputed to have rescued forty people in an avalanche; **Argos:** waited twenty years for the return of Odysseus; **Balto;** a sled dog with life-saving serum for Nome, Alaska; **Krambambuli:** a faithful hunting dog for which a literary monument was written; **Rin Tin Tin:** the German shepherd and animal star of Hollywood; **the Hound of the Baskervilles**, the black monster in the famous Sherlock Holmes mystery.

Beauregard *French for "good-looking"*

Beethoven *The St. Bernard star of the movie* Beethoven

Ben *Beloved son, short for* Benjamin, Benny

Benji *Clever terrier mix in movie series* Benji

Benson *Gentle, mild mannered, well behaved*

Bentley *A flashy, classy, elegant dog*

Bernie *Brave, nickname for* Bernard

Bingo *Childhood song about a dog named B-I-N-G-O*

Biscuit *For the dog who loves treats*

Blackberry *A sweet, black dog*

Blackie *An all black, or mostly black dog, also* Black

Blackjack *A playful black dog that loves games*

Blade *Dashing young male*

Blaze *Fire, a dog with a white blaze on its face*

Blitz *Burst of lightning, energetic dog*

Blizzard *A heavy snowstorm, a white dog with a lot of hair*

Blooper *A funny mistake, good name for a comical dog*

Blue *Dog on children's show* Blues Clues

Bob *A bob tail, or short-tailed dog*

Bobby *Meaning "a great reputation," short for* Robert

Bogart *Movie hero Humphrey Bogart, also* Bogie

Bonkers *Crazy and wild, nuts*

Bonsai *Dwarfed, ornamental tree, good name for a tiny dog*

Bonzer *Australian for "excellent, attractive, pleasing"*

Boo *A sound to frighten or surprise*

Boogie *Lively, dancing, active dog*

Boomer *Strong, bold, outgoing, always returns home, also* Boomerang

Booster *An enthusiastic promoter, increasing power*

Boots *High white socks, or markings, on the hind feet*

Boss *In charge, bossy, dominant personality*

Bourbon *A whiskey, name for a dog with rich brown coloration*

Brando *Actor Marlon Brando*

Brass *For a shiny, brass-colored dog, short for "the brass ring," high ranking*

Brook *The dog that loves water, also* Brooke

Bruno *A large, heavily coated dog, such as a St. Bernard*

Bubba *Slang for "buddy," or "friend"*

Buck *The dog in Jack London's book* The Call of the Wild

Buddy *A close friend and companion*

Buster *Comedian Buster Keaton*

Buzz *The busy body dog*

Caboose *A small dog, a dog that is a bit slow and always last*

Cadbury *Chocolate company in England,* Cad *for short when the dog misbehaves*

Caesar *Ruler of the Roman Empire*

Cairo *Capital of Egypt, good name for a pharaoh hound*

Cajun *Native of Louisiana descended from the French, spicy, also* Cajan

Canopus *Second-brightest star in the sky, 650 light-years from Earth*

Casanova *Italian adventurer, loved by women*

Casey *Baseball player in poem by E. L. Thayer*

Cassidy *Cowboy hero Hopalong Cassidy*

Champ *A winner, a champion*

Chance *Dog hero in the movie* Homeward Bound

Chaos *Greek for "extreme disorder and confusion"*

The Best Names for Princes and Princesses

Diana: Princess of Wales; Apollo: god of light, poetry, and music; Fergie: Duchess of York; Duke: an English noble; Alexander: the great King of Macedonia; Leda: the lover of Zeus; Anastasia: the daughter of the last czar; Jasmine: the princess from Disney's *Aladdin*.

LORD BYRONS BOATSWAIN

The poet Lord Byron thanked Boatswain, his Newfoundland, for his loyalty by having the following carved on its tombstone:

Near this spot are deposited the remains of one who possessed beauty without vanity, strength without insolence, courage without ferocity, and all the virtures of man without his vices. This praise, which would be unmeaning flattery if inscribed over human ashes, is but a just tribute to the memory of Boatswain, a dog who was born at Newfoundland, May 1803, and died at Newstead, November 18, 1808.

Charcoal *Very dark gray or brown, almost black*

Charles *Of French origin, also Charlie or Charley*

Chase *To hunt or follow quickly, good for a hunting dog*

Checkers *The cocker spaniel that belonged to President Nixon*

Chester *A masculine name of old English origin*

Cheyenne *Native American tribe, capital of Wyoming, country dog*

Chico *"Boy" in Spanish*

Chief *Leader of a tribe*

Chili *A hot pepper or hot dish*

Chipper *Lively and cheerful, also Chip, Chips*

Chocolate *Good name for a sweet dog that is rich brown in color*

Chopin *Famous pianist*

Cisco *After the bandit The Cisco Kid*

Clark *William Clark, explorer in the Corps of Discovery (Lewis and Clark)*

Clifford *The big red cartoon dog*

Clyde *Thief, from Bonnie and Clyde*

Cody *Army scout and showman (Buffalo Bill Cody)*

Cognac *A French brandy distilled from wine*

Colombo *Droll detective from the TV series Colombo*

Comet *A heavenly body with a tail*

Cooper *Actor Gary Cooper, writer James Fenimore Cooper*

Copper *Ideal for a reddish brown dog*

Cosmo *Pertaining to the heavens or cosmos*

Cousteau *Famous underwater diver, great for a water dog*

Crackers *Crazy, insane, nutty*

Cruiser *For the dog that loves to ride in the car*

Cupid *God of love in Roman mythology, winged cherub*

Curly *Perfect name for a dog with curly hair*

Cyrano *Cyrano de Bergerac, from the story by Rostand, had a very long nose, good name for a Collie*

Czar *King, ruler, also Tsar*

Daffy *Crazy duck in animated cartoons Daffy Duck*

Dakota *Meaning ally or friend, a group of Native American tribes, also Sioux*

Dallas *From the popular TV drama series Dallas, a major city in Texas*

Dandy *First-rate and very good, also Dandelion*

Dapple *Variegation of spots, mottles, or colors*

Darby *A devoted individual, from the 18th century English verse "Darby and Joan"*

Darcy *Australian champion boxer James Darcy*

Dazzler *A dog that arouses admiration with its brilliant qualities*

Dealer *A gambling dog that takes chances*

Diablo *Spanish for the "devil"*

Diamond *A precious stone, a precious dog*

Digger *Just right for a dog that loves to dig holes*

Dingo *An Australian wild dog*

Dino *Short for "dinosaur"*

Dogbane *A family of poisonous plants*

Domino *A dog with white spots*

Dreamweaver *Creator of dreams, also Dreamer for short*

Duke *A nobleman or prince*

Dustin *Actor Dustin Hoffman*

Dusty *For a dust-colored dog, or a dog that is always dirty*

Dylan *Singer and songwriter Bob Dylan*

Ebony *Deep, dark, black wood*

Eclipse *Famous, outshining, and overshadowing*

Eddie *Nickname for Edward, meaning "guardian," "protector"*

Edsel *An outmoded model Ford car*

E.T. *Extraterrestrial, from the movie E.T.*

Einstein *Genius, scientist Albert Einstein, for a smart dog*

Elmo *Fuzzy character on the TV show Sesame Street*

Elvis *Famous rock star Elvis Presley*

Emery *King or ruler*

Emerson *Poet Ralph Waldo Emerson, classy name*

Ernie *Short for Ernest, German word origin for "resolute"*

The Most Famous Names in Movies and Televsion

Lassie: the most famous collie of all times; Benji: the comical mongrel in *Benji on the Trail*; Lady and Tramp, Disney's mates in the movie bearing their names; Hooch: the slobbering Bordeaux mastiff in *Turner and Hooch*; Beethoven: the St. Bernard in the movie; Petey: the lovable pit bull from the *Little Rascals*.

Fala *The name of President Franklin D. Roosevelt's Scottish terrier*

Felix *Happy, Latin origin*

Fernando *Italian for Ferdinand*

Ferrari *A fast, Italian race car*

Fiat *A fast, sporty dog, named after an Italian sports car*

Figaro *The character in Mozart's opera The Marriage of Figaro*

Firecracker *A loud, explosive dog that loves celebrations*

Flag *Colorful dog, like a banner with colors, commander's flag*

Flambeau *French for a "lighted torch" or "large candlestick"*

Flame *Flickering fire, also a sweetheart*

Flash *A burst or blaze of light*

Flipper *The dolphin in the TV series Flipper*

Flynn *Masculine Irish name, actor Errol Flynn*

Foul Play *Breaking the rules, a good name for a sporting dog. Alternate spelling Fowl Play, ideal for a retriever*

Fox *A clever animal, reddish in color*

Francis *The patron saint of animals*

Freckles *For a dog with small, brownish spots*

Freeway *The terrier in the TV series Hart to Hart*

Freeze Frame *Scene taken from a motion picture to look like a photograph, dramatic effect, good for an active dog*

Friday *A faithful helper, the devoted servant of Robinson Crusoe*

Fritz *German masculine name*

Frost *For a white dog, after the frozen mist, crystalline coating*

Fudge *A sweet, dark dog*

Fuzzy *For the dog that is covered with soft, fine hairs*

Gabriel *An angel, bearer of good news*

Galahad *A pure and noble knight from the King Arthur legend*

Gambler *One who plays games and takes chances for sport*

Garnet *Crystal-like gem found in a variety of red colors*

Garth *Country-western singer Garth Brooks*

Gatsby *The character in* The Great Gatsby, *by F. Scott Fitzgerald*

Genie *A genius, a supernatural form that grants wishes*

Gershwin *American composer and pianist*

Ghirardelli *Top-rate dog, dark in color, like the chocolates*

Gilligan *Shipwrecked character on the TV series* Gilligan's Island

Gizmo *A gadget or a gimmick*

Glengarry *A Scottish cap for men*

Goofy *Mickey Mouse's buddy in animated Disney cartoons*

Graffiti *For a dog with unusual markings, like scribbles on walls*

Gray *A masculine name, the color gray, Gray Dawn the hero collie in the stories by Albert Payson Terhune*

Groucho *One of the Marx Brothers comedy team, for a dog with a moustache*

Gulliver *Main character in the political satire* Gulliver's Travels *by Jonathan Swift*

Gumshoe *A sneaky, stealthy detective, good name for a bloodhound*

Hairy *As in Harry, for a very hairy dog*

Half-pint *Very small*

Hallmark *Genuine mark, stamped in gold or silver, high quality*

Hamlet *The main character in Shakespeare's* Hamlet

Hannibal *General who crossed the Alps to invade Italy in 218 B.C.*

Hansel *From the children's fairy tale "Hansel and Gretel"*

Harlequin *Many colors, also a comic pantomime*

Harley *Harley Davidson, the popular motorcycle*

Harpo *The silent member of the Marx Brothers comedy team*

Hawkeye *For a dog with keen eyesight*

Hemlock *A poisonous plant*

Hercules *In mythology, the incredibly strong son of Zeus*

Hero *For the family pet hero, Greek word meaning "to watch over and protect"*

Hershey *A sweet, chocolate-colored dog, brand of chocolates*

Hobbes *Comic strip character from* Calvin and Hobbes

Holmes *Detective Sherlock Holmes*

Homer *Greek writer, author of* The Iliad *and* The Odyssey

Hooch *The Dogue de Bordeaux that starred with Tom Hanks in* Turner and Hooch

Hooligan *A hoodlum or troublemaker*

The Best Names for Pirates and Adventurers

Robinson: ripe for the island with Daniel Defoe's *Robinson Crusoe*; Vasco: with Vasco da Gama en route to India; Geronimo: famous Apache chief; Gypsy: in need of the wide open sky; Blackbeard: the most notorious pirate of the seas; Columbus: explorer of the new world.

Hopalong *Cowboy hero Hopalong Cassidy*
Hot Rod *Speedy dog, a stripped car rebuilt for speed*
Houdini *Escape artist magician*
Hubert *The bloodhound in the movie* Best in Show
Huckleberry *Tom Sawyer's friend in* Huckleberry Finn *by Mark Twain*
Humdinger *Slang for something excellent or special*
Hummer *A huge dog, after the large, oversized jeeplike vehicle*
Hunter *Good name for a hunting dog*
Hurricane *A storm, violent tropical cyclone*

Icon *For the ultimate dog, an important individual, an image*
Igloo *A white dog or an Eskimo breed, after the Eskimo hut built of blocks of ice*
Indiana Jones *Adventurer, hero, professor, and archaeologist in the Indiana Jones movies*
Indigo *Deep, dark blue, one of seven colors in the rainbow*
Inky *Darkly colored*
IQ *Intelligence quotient, level of intelligence*

Jabberwocky *A nonsense poem of gibberish by Lewis Carroll*
Jackpot *A real winner dog, the highest stakes and winnings*
Jacques *French for John, underwater explorer Jacques Cousteau*
Jaguar *A sports car, also a large, fast feline*
Jason *Means "healer," in Greek mythology the prince who led the Argonauts and found the Golden Fleece*
Jasper *A precious dog named after the green precious stone, also a reddish, yellowish, or brownish quartz*
Jaws *Great name for a dog with a big mouth or big teeth*
Jet *For a very fast, or very dark dog*
Jethro *Rock group Jethro Tull*
Jingles *A happy dog, light, ringing sounds, like bells*

Jinx *Something that brings bad luck*
Jitters *For the nervous dog that is always moving about, nervous*
Jock *A sporty, athletic individual*
Joker *A dog that has a sense of humor and plays tricks*
Jolly *High spirits and good humor, happy*
Jordache *Fashion designer*
Jumbo *Large size, very big*
Junior *Smaller, younger*
Jupiter *The god of all gods in Roman mythology, also the largest planet in our solar system*

K. C. *Short for Casey, Kasey*
Karate *One of the martial arts, good name for an Asian-breed dog*
Kent *Clark Kent, mild-mannered reporter who was actually Superman*
Kermit *The frog on the TV show* Sesame Street

THE TOP TEN FOR MALE DOGS

Max: short for Maximilian, meaning great; **Jake**: slang for all right or fine; **Buddy**: your best pal and confidant; **Bailey**: an after-dinner liqueur from Ireland; **Sam** or **Sammy**: a great one for decades; **Rocky**: champion boxer from the movies; **Buster**: comedian Buster Keaton, a dog to make you smile; **Casey**: at the bat, fictional baseball player; **Cody**: "Buffalo" Bill Cody, of the wild west; **Duke**: a royal name for an honorable pet.

The Most Enchanting Names from Fairy Tales and Fables

Aladdin: authentic only with a magic lamp in *The Arabian Nights*; Cinderella: from the bewitching fairy tale; Gretel: always with her Hansel in the Brothers Grimm story; Ali: a certain fellow named Baba and the forty thieves; Tinkerbell: the sprightly fairy in the tale of Peter Pan; Puck: the mischievous fairy in Shakespeare; Rapunzel: trapped in a tower with her long, flowing hair.

Kibbles *Good name for an eager eater*

Kicker *A surprising end or an ironic twist*

Kilroy *Popular European graffiti in the 1940s "Kilroy was here!"*

King *Ruler, royalty*

Kirby *Irish name, also Kerby*

Kirk *Captain Kirk of the TV series* Star Trek

Kiwi *A native of New Zealand, also a small, green fruit*

Knickknack *A small, decorative ornament*

Knight *A servant of the king of high military rank*

Kodak *For the dog that "should be in pictures" and has a lot of "Kodak moments"*

Kodiak *For a giant, strong dog, after the large Alaskan bear*

Kooky *Silly, ridiculous, eccentric*

Korbel *A dog with extravagant tastes, a brand of champagne*

Kudos *Praise, fame, admiration, glory*

Kumquat *Small orange fruit, ideal Chinese name for an Asian-breed dog*

Lad *The hero collie in Albert Payson Terhune's novels.*

Lafayette *Marquis de Lafayette, French general who fought in the American Revolution with his friend President George Washington*

Lamborghini *An expensive and fast dog, expensive Italian sports car*

Lancelot *Knight of the Round Table in King Arthur's legend*

Langley *The computer nerd in the TV series* The X-Files

Lefty *A left-hander, popular nickname*

Legacy *Value handed down from an ancestor*

Legend *Story or myth lasting generations*

Lenny *Short for Leonard, meaning "strong as a lion"*

Leonardo *Famous artist Leonardo da Vinci, Italian for Leonard*

Leopold *Emperor of the Roman Empire*

Lexy *Short, attractive name, from Lexicon, an ancient language*

Liaison *A link, a love affair*

Licorice *For a sweet black or red dog, after the candy*

Linus *Charlie Brown's friend in the comic strip* Peanuts *by Charles Schulz*

Lion *Large, powerful feline considered "king of the beasts"*

Live Wire *Energetic individual, a wire carrying an electrical current*

Livingston *Scottish explorer in Africa found by Sir Henry Morton Stanley*

Lobo *Spanish, meaning "wolf"*

Loco *Spanish for "crazy" or "demented"*

Logan *The highest mountain range in Canada*

Loki *God of fires in Norwegian legend*

London *The capital of the United Kingdom*

Long Shot *A slight chance of winning, so rewards are greater in a bet*

Lucky *Having good fortune or bringing good luck*

Mac the Nipper *Play on words for Jack the Ripper*

Macbeth *Scottish tartan, also the character in Shakespeare's play* Macbeth

Macho *Spanish for "strong and courageous male"*

27

THE PRESIDENT'S TERRIER

During his term in office, President Franklin D. Roosevelt received a gift from a relative—a Scottish terrier puppy. Although his wife Eleanor thought the White House was not the best home for a pet, Fala (the puppy's name) quickly found a place in the President's heart and accompanied him everywhere. Fala is buried near his master at Hyde Park, New York.

Magic *Mysterious illusions, spells, charms*

Magnum *From the TV crime series* Magnum PI

Marco *Spanish for Marcus, meaning "Mars"*

Marmaduke *The name of the Great Dane in the* Marmaduke *comic series*

Mars *Roman mythology god of war, the red planet*

Max *Meaning "great," short for Maximilian*

Maximus *Greatest, biggest, from Latin*

Mephisto *Diabolical, crafty, powerful*

Merlin *Legendary magician who helped King Arthur*

Michelangelo *Famous sculptor, painter, and architect*

Micky *Irish nickname for Michael, also Mickey, Mikie*

Milo *The hero cat in the movie* Milo and Otis

Minimax *Original combination of little and big*

Mister *Masculine title, as in Mr. Spock*

Mitch *English masculine name*

Moby *The whale in Herman Melville's novel* Moby Dick

Molière *French dramatist, writer*

Mongrel *A dog of mixed breeds*

Monsoon *Powerful, seasonal wind of the Indian Ocean and Asia*

Moocher *A dog who begs for food, also Mooch*

Moonbeam *A ray of moonlight, also Moonlight, Moon for short*

Moonshine *Illegally distilled whiskey*

Motley *Patches of many colors*

Mulder *The brilliant FBI agent in the TV series* The X-Files

Muppet *A puppet from the TV series* The Muppets

Murphy *An Irish masculine name,* Murphy's Law

Mutt *A dog of mixed breeds,* Mutt and Jeff *comic series*

Nachos *Mexican snack dish, good name for a Chihuahua*

Nairobi *Capital of Kenya, in Africa*

Napoleon *Emperor of France and military leader*

Neil *The alcoholic St. Bernard on the TV series* Topper

Neptune *God of the sea in Roman mythology*

Nibbles *Also Nibble, or Nibbler*

Nick *Victory, short for Nicholas*

Nipper *The famous terrier on the RCA Victor labels*

Noah *Hebrew masculine name meaning "rest and comfort"*

Nobel *Famous, illustrious, great character*

Noggin *A small cup to measure liquor; nickname for head*

Nomad *A wanderer, for the dog that likes to wander*

Nugget *A chunk of gold, gold colored*

Odysseus *Hero in Homer's epic story* The Odyssey

Ollie *Short for Oliver*

Omega *From Greek, meaning "great"*

Omen *Something that foretells a future event*

Onyx *Having colored layers, an agate, semiprecious stone*

Opie *Diminutive, Ron Howard's little boy character on the* Andy Griffith Show

Oregano *Fragrant herb used in cooking*

Oreo *A popular black-and-white cookie*

Orion *In Roman mythology, a hunter that was placed in the heavens as a constellation*

Oscar *The* Sesame Street *character who lives in a trash can, an award*

Othello *Main character in the Shakespearean tragedy* Othello

Otis *The adventuresome pug in the movie* Milo and Otis

Pablo *Spanish for Paul*

Paddy *Nickname for English name Patrick*

Paint *A piebald or pinto pattern*

Paisano *Spanish for "comrade" or "friend"*

Pan *In Greek mythology, the god of fields, forests, and wild animals*

Patton *American General George Patton during World War II*

Pavarotti *Italian opera singer Luciano Pavarotti*

Peanuts *Cartoon strip by Charles Schulz, Peanut for a small dog*

Pecos *Pecos Bill, folklore cowboy who dug the Rio Grande*

Pedro *Spanish for Peter*

Pee Wee *A tiny dog*

Pepe *Romantic skunk in cartoon series* Pepe le Pew

Pepper *Good name for a black dog*

Percy *Short for Percival, name of dog in Disney's* Pocahontas

Petey *The dog in the movie* The Little Rascals

Pharoah *King of Egypt in ancient times*

Picasso *Spanish artist Pablo Picasso*

Pierre *French for Peter*

Pinto *Patches of white and another color such as brown or black*

Plato *Greek philosopher*

Pluto *Mickey Mouse's dog in Disney cartoons*

Pocket *Small enough to fit in a pocket*

Poochie *Term of endearment for a dog*

Polo *Fashion label, also Venetian traveler Marco Polo*

Pongo *Hero Dalmatian in Disney's* 101 Dalmatians

Popeye *Hero sailor in the cartoon series* Popeye

Poseidon *God of the sea and horses in Greek mythology*

Prince *Royalty, handsome, future king*

Puck *Character from Shakespeare's* A Midsummer Night's Dream

The Funniest Names from Comics and Cartoons

Bluto: Popeye's nemesis and admirer of Olive Oil; Donald: a drake named Donald Duck who conquers the world; Minnie: the wife at the side of Mickey Mouse; Scooby Doo: the clumsy Great Dane who solves mysteries; Popeye: the classic sailor and spinach nibbler; Snoopy: Charlie Brown's independent beagle.

Quantum *Quantum leap, change in energy*
Quincy *English name, Quincy Jones composer*
Quixote *Don Quixote, the idealist in the writings of Miguel de Cervantes*

Radar *A dog that locates and follows everywhere*
Ramses *Egyptian Pharaoh*
Rebel *For the dog that resists authority*
Red *Good name for a dog with reddish hair*
Rembrandt *Dutch artist and painter*
Remington *Remington Steele, also Remy*
Remus *In Roman mythology, the twin brother of Romulus, nursed by a wolf*
Reno *Gambling city in Nevada*
Rex *National champion sheepdog in the movie* Babe, *means "king"*
Rhett *Rhett Butler, dashing character in Margaret Mitchell's* Gone with the Wind
Riley *Valiant, also Reilly and O'Riley*

Ringleader *A leader, also a clownish troublemaker*
Ringo *Famous drummer in the rock group The Beatles*
Rin Tin Tin *German shepherd from TV series* The Adventures of Rin Tin Tin
Ripley *Means "from the echo valley," good name for a dog that is hard to believe, Ripley's Believe It or Not museum*

Robin *The legends of Robin Hood; also Batman's sidekick in comics and movies*
Rocky *Boxer in the movie series* Rocky
Rojo *Spanish for "red"*
Romeo *From Shakespeare's tragic love story* Romeo and Juliet
Romulus *In Roman mythology, the first king of Rome and twin brother of Remus, both nursed by a wolf*
Rossini *Means "noble and proud," also composer Rossini*
Rowdy *Rough and disorderly, Rowdy Yates on TV series* Rawhide
Roy *Celtic name for "red"; also the cowboy Roy Rogers*
Rusty *Great name for a dog with brownish red coloration*

PAVLOV'S DOGS

More than a hundred years ago Ivan Petrovitch Pavlov wrote about his classic experiment on conditioned reflexes: Every time his test dogs were fed, Pavlov had a bell rung. Whereas the bell previously had no meaning, after only a few occurrences it stimulated the dogs to salivate in the expectation of being fed. Soon the bell alone triggered this reaction.

Sampson *For a strong dog with long hair, also Samson*
Satchmo *Jazz musician Louis "Satchmo" Armstrong*
Scamp *Mischievous rascal*
Scooby *Great Dane in the cartoon* Scooby-Doo
Scotty *Good name for a terrier, Scotty from* Star Trek
Scout *For an investigative dog*
Shadow *A dog that follows everywhere*
Shaka *Zulu warrior chief*
Shakespeare *England's greatest playwright, William Shakespeare*
Shamrock *A good-luck dog, good for an Irish breed*
Shane *From the award-winning movie* Shane
Shep *A shepherd dog*
Sherlock *Sherlock Holmes, famous detective*
Shiloh *Hebrew name for "place of peace"*
Silver *Ideal name for a silvery dog*
Sirius *The dog star*
Sky *For a bluish gray dog, short for Skylar*
Smokey *Smoke color, grayish black, also Smoky*
Snoopy *The beagle in the comic strip* Peanuts *by Charles Schulz*
Soccer *Name of the Jack Russell terrier in real life that stars in the TV series* Wishbone
Socrates *Greek philosopher*
Sparky *Dashing and gallant*
Spartacus *Roman gladiator*
Speck *Pee-Wee Herman's dog in* Pee-Wee's Big Adventure
Speedy *Speedy Gonzales, "the fastest mouse in Mexico"* Looney

The Most Impressive **Names** for **Machos** und **Maestros**

Achilles: the great hero of Troy; Alpha: the number-one place in the Greek alphabet and in life; Merlin: the sorcerer of the English sagas; Attila: ideally not as warlike as the king of the Huns; Hannibal: for dogs with leadership qualities; Hercules: the ultra-strong dog of the house; Patton: a strong leader; Zeus: the father of the gods in Greek mythology.

Toons cartoon character, ideal name for a Chihuahua or fast dog
Spock *Mr. Spock, character on TV series* Star Trek
Spot *Dick and Jane's dog, "See Spot run!"*
Spuds *Spuds McKenzie, the bull terrier in the beer commercials*
Suess *Dr. Seuss, author of children's stories*

Tango *South American dance*
Tanner *Cowboy name, leather maker*
Teddy *Short for Edward, meaning "guardian," also a cuddly teddy bear*
Tex *Short for Texan, from Texas*
Thor *Norse mythology, the god of thunder and strength*
Titan *Great size, strength, power*
Toby *Short for Tobias, meaning "precious"*
Tonto *Faithful Native American companion of the Lone Ranger*

Topper *The very best, tops, also a joke*
Toto *Dorothy's cairn terrier in the Baum classic* The Wizard of Oz
Tracker *Perfect name for a tracking hound*
Tramp *Hero dog in Disney's animated movie* Lady and the Tramp
Trapper *Good name for a hunting dog*
Tritan *God of the sea in Greek mythology*
Trooper *Ideal for a working or service dog*
Trouble *A name for the dog that is often in trouble, also Troubles*
Truman *Jim Carrey's character in the movie* The Truman Show, *also a United States president*
Trusty *Loyal, devoted, reliable*
Turbo *Fast, powerful, supercharged*

31

Underdog *Animated cartoon series of Superman-like hero canine*
Ulysses *Same as Odysseus, the hero in Homer's* The Odyssey

Vader *Darth Vader from the movie* Star Wars
Valentine *Sweetheart*
Van Gogh *Famous painter*
Verdi *Italian opera composer*
Viking *Scandinavian sea rover, pirate*

Waldo *Ruler, also game Where's Waldo?*
Wallace *Alfred Russel Wallace, naturalist, also Wally*
Watson *Friend of detective Sherlock Holmes*
Weenie *Teeny, tiny, small*
Whammo *Exclamation, sudden surprise*
Whirligig *A toy that moves in circles*
Whiskey *Strong alcoholic liquor*
White Fang *Book by Jack London*
Widget *A hypothetical gadget*

Wiley *Wile E. Coyote animated cartoon character*
Willie *Short for William, meaning "protection"*
Wishbone *The Jack Russell terrier on the TV series* Wishbone
Wolf *Rip Van Winkle's dog*
Wolfgang *Composer Wolfgang Amadeus Mozart*
Wolverine *main character in the X-Men movies, a small carnivorous mammal*
Won Ton *A Chinese dumpling, good name for Asian-breed dog*
Wrangler *Cowboy, brand of blue jeans*
Wrinkles *Ideal for a shar-pei, bulldog, or other wrinkly dog*
Wyoming *A U.S. state*

Xeno *Greek for "foreigner" or "stranger"*
Xerxes *A Persian king*

Yankee *Native of the United States, also Yankee Doodle*
Yodel *Name of sled dog in the movie* Snow Dogs
Yogi *Animated cartoon character Yogi Bear*
Yukon *Territory in Canada*

Zachariah *Means "remembered," also Zac, Zack, or Zak for short*
Zappa *Rock music star Frank Zappa*
Zeus *Doberman pinscher in TV series* Magnum P.I., *in Greek mythology ruler of the gods*
Zip *The Collie in the children's book series* The Happy Hollisters
Zorro *Legendary masked hero, Spanish for "fox"*
Zvezdochka *Russian for "little star," name of the dog sent into space by the Russians*

The Best Names for Friends and Chums

Simon and Garfunkel: singing duo; Siegfried and Roy: notable lion tamers; Bonnie and Clyde: the norotious crime duo of the 1930s; Bert and Ernie: friends and roommates from the children's show *Sesame Street*; Felix and Oscar: opposites from the TV series *The Odd Couple*.

The Best Names
for Female Dogs

Abby *Short for Abigail*
Aida *Romantic, extravagant, Verdi's opera* Aida
Aja *From Italian meaning "educated," also a good name for Asiatic breeds (Pekingese, shih tzu, Lhasa apso)*
Akira *Japanese for "intelligent and bright"*
Alba *Latin for "white"*
Alexa *World traveler and worldly wise, short for Alexandria*
Alyeska *A mountain in Alaska*
Alice *Meaning "truth," also main character in* Alice in Wonderland *by Lewis Carroll, also Alicia*
Alma *Meaning "origin" or "source"*
Alva *A feminine Swedish name*
Amalie *Variation of Amelia*
Amanda *A dog to light up your life, Mandy or Mandi for short*
Amber *A deep, reddish color*
Ambrosia *Immortal and divine or food of the gods, also David Bowie's dog in the movie* Labyrinth
Amelia *Very feminine, yet adventurous*
Amélie *French version of Amelia*

The Best Names
for Couples and Partners

Romeo and Juliet: the most beautiful love of all times; Caesar and Cleo(patra): simply classic; Fred and Ginger: graceful dancing partners; Scarlett and Rhett: eternal lovers from *Gone with the Wind*; Robin (Hood) and Marion: the flaming arrow of love; Napoleon and Josephine: deep feelings

Amiga *A good friend and companion*
Amy *Loved one, in French, aimée*
Anastasia *Perfect for the canine princess*
Angel *Always good, kind, lovable, perfectly well behaved*
Angelina *Another form of Angel, also Angela, Angie*
Anika *Russian for Annie*
Annie *Grace, also Anna*
Aphrodite *Goddess of love in Greek mythology*
Apricot *Sweet, light orange fruit*
April *Ideal for a dog born in the springtime or month of April*

Aquarius *Pertaining to water, ideal for a water dog*
Aria *Vocal solo in an opera*
Ariel *The airy spirit in Shakespeare's* The Tempest
Aries *A constellation, the first sign of the zodiac*
Asta *The wire-haired fox terrier that belonged to Nick and Nora Charles in the film series* The Thin Man
Astra *Like a star*
Athena *Greek goddess of wisdom and art*
Audrey *Strong and noble*
Aura *Feeling, sensation, impression*

Autumn *Born in the fall, or colored shades of autumn*
Azalea *A plant that produces numerous, colorful flowers*

Babe *Slang for a very attractive individual*
Babette *French name, endearment*
Babushka *Term of endearment*
Baby *Very young, innocent*
Ballet *A graceful dance*
Bangle *A decorative bracelet*
Barbie *Nickname for Barbara*
Bazooka *A popular bubble gum*
Beauty *Extremely attractive, beautiful*
Bebe *Very small, also French for baby*
Becky *Someone captivating, short for Rebecca*
Begonia *A tropical plant with clusters of flowers*
Belladonna *A beautiful lady, also a poisonous plant*
Belle *French for "very pretty," also Bella*

Bessy *Short for Elizabeth, also Bess or Bessie*
Bianca *White or very light colored*
Bibi *Short for Barbara*
Bijou *French for "jewel"*
Birdie *English nickname meaning "little bird"*
Bitsy *Something small, itsy bitsy*
Bliss *Happiness, joy*
Blithe *Cheerful, carefree, gleaming*
Blondie *Blonde colored, also a rock singer from the 1980s*
Blossom *Flowers, buds, and blooms in a cluster*
Bo *Actress Bo Derek from the movie Ten*
Bombshell *A sudden surprise*
Bonbon *A French candy*
Bonita *Spanish for "very pretty"*
Bonnie *Good, sweet, nice*
Bora *Scandanavian name for "friend"*
Bordeaux *An excellent wine from the Bordeaux region of France*

Bouquet *A cluster of flowers*
Brandy *A liquor, a deep, dark, golden color*
Brazen *Copper in color, bold*
Bree *Strong, short for Brianna*
Breezy *Light, airy, like the breeze*
Bridget *English name*
Brit *Celtic word meaning "speckled, varicolored"*
Brittany *Region in France, Britt for short*
Brownie *Good name for a sweet, dark, chocolate-colored dog*
Bubbles *A bubbly personality, lively, happy*
Buff *A pale color, also Buffy*
Bunny *Baby rabbit, good name for a small, cuddly dog*
Burgundy *Deep purplish color, region of France famous for wines*
Buttercup *Bright yellow flower*
Butterscotch *A light yellow-brown mixture of brown sugar and butter, perfect name for butterscotch-colored dog with a sweet personality*
Buttons *An ideal name for a small, bright, lively dog*

Cabaret *Entertainment with dancing and singing*
Callie *Nickname for Caroline*
Calliope *A beautiful voice, a keyboard instrument similar to an organ, unusual and pretty-sounding feminine name*
Calypso *The sea nymph who keeps Odysseus on her island in Homer's The Odyssey*

Classical Names from Mythology

Goliath: the giant killed by David; Flora: the goddess of springtime; Lady Godiva: nude, on horseback, through London; Mars: the Roman god of war; Odysseus: gone on a long journey of wandering; Aphrodite: Greek goddess of love; Athena: Zeus' daughter and goddess of war; Pandora: one with a curious nature.

LOVE COMES WITH SPAGHETTI

Her name is Lady and she is a cocker spaniel from the best house; he is an adventurous tramp, and that's his name. As the two of them eat spaghetti, things click between them. And everything that starts off sad turns out well. It took four full years for 150 illustrators to produce the 110,000 images for Disney's animated masterpiece *Lady and the Tramp*.

Camille *French name for "integrity and perfect character"*
Candy *A sweet treat*
Caramel *Sweet name for a brown or honey-colored dog*
Carmen *Seductive main character in Bizet's opera* Carmen
Cassy *Short for the English name Cassandra*
Chablis *A white wine, originally from Chablis, France*
Champagne *A white wine regarded as a symbol of luxury*
Chantilly *A type of lace, originally from Chantilly, France*
Charade *A game acted out in pantomime, great name for a playful dog*
Charlotte *French feminine name for Charles*
Charm *Perfect for an enchanting, attractive, magical dog*
Chère *French for "dear," also Cherie, Cher*

Chica *Spanish for "little girl"*
Chiffon *Light, fancy, sweet, as in chiffon lace or chiffon pie*
Cinder *A coal that is still burning but not flaming, a good name for a dark-colored dog, also short for Cinderella*
Cinnamon *A spice used for desserts, fun name for a yellowish brown dog*

Cleo *Short for Cleopatra, the Basset Hound on the TV series* The People's Choice
Cloudy *Great name for a dog with patches of white in the coat*
Cocoa *Perfect name for a richly colored brown dog*
Cookie *Someone clever, as in "a smart cookie," a sweet treat*
Coquette *A flirt*
Crystal *Clear and brilliant, pure*
Cuddles *Lovable, huggable, likes to snuggle*

Daffodil *A yellow flower*
Daisy *A flower, also Donald Duck's girlfriend*
Dancer *A dog that moves lightly, prances*
Dandelion *French* dent de lion *meaning "tooth of a lion," a flower*
Daphne *A nymph in Greek mythology who escaped from Apollo*
Darcy *Short, attractive, feminine name, variation Darcie*
Darla *A nickname for Darling*
Darling *Something very dear, cherished, and loved, a river in Australia*
Dawn *Early morning, the famous blue-merle collie in Albert Payson Terhune's story* Gray Dawn
Dee Dee *A nickname, also short for Diane or Diana*
Déjà Vu *The feeling of having already had an experience that is actually new, also Déjà, or for a silvery or blue-merle dog, Déjà Blue*

35

Delia *Feminine form of Delios, also an island in the Aegean Sea*
Demitasse *Small cup of black coffee, French for "half cup"*
Destiny *Fate, intended purpose, from French "destinee"*
Dice *Small white cubes with black spots, used for playing games*
Dido *Mischievous prank or caper, New Age singer*
Dinkum *Australian slang meaning "true, genuine, or real"*
Diva *Prima donna, leading female singer in an opera*
Dixie *The southern states of the United States*
Dizzy *Silly, foolish, giddy, confused, bewildered*
Dolly *Nickname for Dorothy, young, pretty, lovable*
Duchess *Nobility and rank, also Duchesse*

Echo *Reflection of sound*
Éclair *An oblong French pastry filled with cream, also Claire*
Edelweiss *Small, white flower as in the song "Edelweiss"*
Eden *A wonderful place or garden*
Ella *Nickname for Eleanor, also Ellie*
Elsie *Derived from Alice or Elizabeth, also Elsa*
Elvira *Spanish feminine name*
Elysian *Happy, delightful, blissful*
Ember *The glowing remains among ashes in a fire, a dog with a glowing personality*
Emily *Feminine name for Emil, Roman origin*

The Best Names for Baby Boomers and Mommy's Sweetheart

Babushka (Babu): a Russian name of endearment; Chérie: my little darling; Honey: sweet to the taste; Barbie: not just for dolls; Snuggles: the mushy pet; Buddy: a faithful friend all through life; Mogli: after Rudyard Kipling's lovable youth in the *Jungle Book*; Sweet Pea: the baby from the cartoon *Popeye*.

Emma *Emma Peel, the fictitious secret agent, also Emmy*
Esmeralda *The young woman in Victor Hugo's story* The Hunchback of Notre Dame
Eunice *A good victory, of Greek origin*

Fabergé *A brand of perfume*
Faith *Feminine name, belief, trust, confidence*
Fajita *A type of Mexican food*
Fanny *Feminine nickname for Frances, French word origin*
Fantasia *A musical composition, also Disney's movie*
Fawn *Pale yellowish brown, a very young deer*
Feather *Soft, lightweight, feathery*
Feisty *An energetic, lively dog full of spirit*
Fendi *Fashion designer*
Fergie *Nickname for Sarah Ferguson*

Fern *A nonflowering plant with fronds*
Fifi *French feminine name*
Firefly *A winged beetle active at night that glows*
Flair *A natural talent or ability, stylish, dashing*
Fleur *French for "flower"*
Flirt *To play at love*
Flora *In Roman mythology, the goddess of flowers*
Flossy *Like light and fluffy, stylish or fancy, also Flossie*
Flower *Flowers made of petals and stems, usually brightly colored*
Flutterby *A mix that sounds like "butterfly"*
Fly *The mother border collie in the movie* Babe
Folly *Foolishness, silliness*
Foxglove *A poisonous flowering plant that produces digitalis*
Foxy *Clever, attractive, seductive, or reddish brown color*
Fraise *French for "strawberry"*

Frappé *A partly frozen, iced dessert*
Frostie *Frost, ice, cold and white, also Frosty*

Gabby *Short for Gabriella, named after the archangel Gabriel*
Gem *A precious stone, also Gemma*
Georgia *Feminine for George, songs "Georgia on My Mind"; also a southern state in the United States*
Giggles *Laughs, a series of silly high-pitched laughs*
Gigi *Promise or pledge, short for Gilberta*
Gina *Italian feminine name, short for Gianna*
Ginger *A spice plant that produces beautiful flowers, famous dancer Ginger Rogers*
Gingersnap *A cookie made from ginger, good name for a golden, sassy dog (or one that snaps or nips!)*
Giselle *From the romantic ballet Giselle*
Givenchy *Fashion designer*
Gloria *Great honor and praise, also Glory*
Godiva *Lady Godiva rode naked through Coventry to plead her case for lower taxes; also a brand of chocolates*
Goldie *A golden color, short for Goldilocks of "Goldilocks and the Three Bears"*
Gracie *Graceful, elegant, classy*
Grace Note *A very short note used to embellish musical compositions*
Greta *A pearl, short for Margaret, also Gretta and Gretchen*
Gretel *From the children's fairy tale "Hansel and Gretel"*
Guinevere *The queen wife of King Arthur, means "white phantom"*
Gumdrop *A colorful chewy candy, good name for a small, colorful dog*
Gummie Bear *A chewy, sweet candy in various colors, shaped like little bears*
Gussie *Nickname for Augusta, also Gussy*
Gypsy *Wandering fortuneteller, musician*

Halley *Halley's comet, also Haley*
Hanna *Short for Joanna, also Hannah, means "blossom"*
Happy *Content, carefree, pleased*
Harmony *Pleasant sounding tones in music*

THE TOP TEN FOR FEMALE DOGS

Abby: short for Abigail; **Daisy:** a favorite flower; **Ginger:** for the dog with a little spice; **Lady:** for the sophisticated pet; **Lucy:** uncomplicated and cute; **Maggie:** nickname for Margaret; **Missy:** an endearment for young miss; **Sandy:** great for a yellow or blonde-colored dog; **Princess:** the spoiled lady, who gets what she wants; **Zoe:** a fun and simple name.

Isabella *The Spanish queen who funded Columbus's voyage*
Isis *The Egyptian goddess of fertility*
Ivory *White, precious material from the tusks of elephants*
Ivy *A trailing, climbing, decorative vine*

Jackie *Nickname for French name Jacqueline*
Jade *Green, a precious stone used for jewelry*
Janie *Nickname for French name Jeanne*
Jasmine *A tropical plant with fragrant flowers*
Java *A great name for a dark, coffee-colored dog*
Jazzabelle *Enliven, embellish, jazzy, play on words for Jezebel*

Hazel *Light yellow brown color*
Heather *A Scottish plant with bell-shaped, purple-pink flowers*
Heidi *One of the dachshunds in Disney's* The Ugly Dachshund
Helen *Helen of Troy, the beautiful queen whose abduction caused the Trojan War*
Henna *A plant with red or white flowers used to tint hair auburn or reddish brown*
Hilda *Short for German Brunhilda, also Hildy*
Holly *A small shrub with bright red berries used as holiday ornaments*
Hollywood *Home of movie studios and movie stars, variation Holly Would!*
Honey *Cute name for a sweet, honey-colored dog, one that "sticks" close by*
Honeybee *A bee that makes honey from plant nectar, a busy little dog*
Hope *Feminine name meaning "trust and reliance"*
Houlihan *Nurse Hotlips in the TV series* MASH

Ida *Old English for "prosperous"*
India *Large region of southern Asia*
Ingrid *Feminine Scandinavian name*
Irene *In Greek mythology, the goddess of peace*
Iris *In Greek mythology, the goddess of the rainbow*

BREED TYPECASTING—THE BAD AND THE GOOD

In the 1980s, the movie *Cujo*, based on the Stephen King novel, portrayed the St. Bernard breed as a giant canine terror. It was almost 20 years later, with the success of the movie *Beethoven*, that the St. Bernard's reputation as a lovable, if not extra large, pet was restored.

The Best Names for Shy Dogs and Sleeping Beauties

Fifi: fitting for small, fresh scamps; Tiffany: to be guarded like a precious jewel; Snowflake: the pampered pet; Little One: always gets her way; Sasha: just right for a lively little pest; Sweetie: who can be angry with such a little darling; Lulu: for capricious girl dogs with their own ideas about things.

Jellybean *A sugary bean-shaped colorful candy, perfect name for a chubby, round dog*

Jenny *Nickname for Jennifer, also Jennie*

Jessie *Short for the Hebrew name Jessica*

Jewel *Precious, valuable, gem*

Jill *A sweetheart, from the nursery rhyme "Jack and Jill"*

Jodie *English name, short for Johanna*

Jonquil *French for "daffodil" or narcissus flowering plant*

Josephine *Napoleon's wife, the French empress*

Joy *A happy, delightful dog*

Joyce *Latin derivative meaning "to be merry"*

Jubilee *A celebration*

Juliet *The heroine in Shakespeare's* Romeo and Juliet

June Bug *A beetle that appears in May and June*

Karen *Nordic name for Karin*

Karma *Fate, destiny*

Katie *Nickname for Katherine or Catherine, also Kitty*

Katydid *For the dog that's always doing something, a fun play on words is "Katy did!"*

Keepsake *Kept for the memories, special and precious*

Kelly *A feminine Irish name*

Kenya *A country in Africa*

Kerry *A county in Ireland*

Kiss *Sign of affection, love*

Lacey *Popular feminine name, a fine lace in ornamental designs*

Lady *The cocker spaniel in Disney's animated cartoon movie* Lady and the Tramp

Ladybug *A bright-colored, tiny beetle*

Ladylove *Sweetheart*

Lamb *Gentle, innocent, loved, also term of endearment Lambkin*

Lanai *One of the Hawaiian islands, also Lana*

Lanner *A female hawk*

Lantana *A shrubby plant with small, colorful flowers*

Lara *Short for Larissa*

Lark *To frolic and play, a spree or prank, a singing bird*

Lassie *The famous collie in* Lassie, *the book by Eric Knight*

Laura *Variation on Laurentius, feminine of Laurence*

Leah *Short, feminine name, also Lea*

Lee *Short for Leslie*

Libby *Endearment for loved one*

Liberty *Freedom*

Liesel *Pronounced Lee-sel, short for Elizabeth*

Lightning Bug *Firefly*

Lilac *Plant with multiple, tiny, fragrant flowers*

Lillie Langtry *Popular English actress (1852–1929)*

Limelight *A brilliant light, a spotlight for an actor*

Limerick *A nonsense poem*

Limoges *A fine porcelain from Limoges, France*

Lindsay *Old English name, also Lindsey*

Liv *Norwegian name, actress Liv Ullmann*

Liz *Short for Elizabeth, also Lizzy or Lizzie*

Lola *Spanish, short for Dolores, also Lolita*

Lollipop *A candy sucker on a stick, also Lolli or Lolly*

Loretta *Pet name for Lora*

Lorna Doone *A cookie named after the romance novel by R. D. Blackmore*

39

Lorraine *Region of northeastern France*
Lottery *A game of chance*
Lotus *A water lily, a fruit that causes dreaminess*
Lovebug *Term of endearment, small flying bug*
Lucy *Nickname for Lucille, also Lucinda*
Lullaby *Sweet song to lull a baby to sleep*
Lulu *Slang for "beautiful girl," short for Louise*
Luna *Roman goddess of the moon*
Lynn *English name short for Linda or Carolyn*

Mabel *From Latin* amabilis, *meaning* lovable
Maddie *Feminine name, short for Magdalena*
Madeline *Variation of Magdalene, Greek feminine name*
Madge *Short for Margaret*
Madonna *Female rock singer*
Maggie *Short for Margaret*
Maisy *English feminine name*
Maleah *Unique combination of May and Leah*
Maliblue *Play on words from Malibu, good for a silvery or bluish-colored dog*
Mandi *Short for the English name Amanda, also Mandy*
Marbles *A marbling pattern, streaked and mottled*
Mardi Gras *Carnival, celebration*
Margarita *A pearl, an alcoholic drink*
Margot *French for Margo*

The Most Outstanding Names for Smart Dogs

Smarty: anyone with a name like that must be clever; Einstein: for real intellectuals; Sherlock: the master detective by Sir Arthur Conan Doyle; Jeannie with magical powers, like the bewitching Jeannie of the television series; Socrates: the great symbol of the philosophers; Noble: A dog of excellence in many fields; Gates: for a dog rich with promise.

Mariah *Fom the Broadway hit* Paint Your Wagon; *singer Mariah Carey*
Marian *Robin Hood's lady friend*
Marmalade *Great name for a yellowish orange-colored dog with a tart personality*
Marshmallow *The perfect name for a soft, white, sweet, cuddly dog*
Mata Hari *Famous exotic dancer accused of spying*
Matilda *Mathilde in German, slang for "kangaroo" in Australia*
Maxine *Feminine name for Max*
May *Spring month, also short for Mary or Margaret*
Maya *Hindu goddess, an illusion*
Megan *Meaning "great, mighty," of Greek origin*

Melanie *From the Greek word for "black"*
Melinda *Tender, delicate*
Melody *A pleasing song*
Mercedes *Spanish feminine name, also a luxury car*
Merle *A blend of colors, marbling, as in blue merle or red merle*
Merry *Happy, full of fun and laughter*
Mia *Italian feminine name*
Mille Fleurs *A thousand flowers, a tapestry design*
Millicent *Strong, work, nickname Millie*
Mimi *Affectionate name*
Mimosa *A genus of trees and plant with small, colorful flowers*
Mindy *Nickname, also short for Melinda*
Mink *A small animal with luxurious fur*

Minnie *Very small or miniature, Mickey Mouse's girlfriend Minnie Mouse in the Disney animated cartoon series*

Missy *Endearment for "young miss," also Missie*

Mistletoe *Ornamental holiday plant*

Mistral *Strong winds that blow over the Mediterranean coast of France*

Misty *Fine vapor, as in a mist of perfume*

Mocha *Chocolate-flavored coffee, color of mocha*

Molasses *For a dark-colored, very sweet dog, or for a dog that is, according to the old expression, "as slow as molasses in winter"*

Molly *Nickname for Mary*

Mona *Means "noble," also da Vinci's painting* Mona Lisa

Moonflower *Tropical twining vine that blooms at night*

Moonlight *Soft light of the moon*

Moonshadow *"I'm being followed by a moonshadow" lyrics from Cat Stevens song "Moonshadow"*

Moppet *Term of endearment, a rag doll*

Mosaic *Artwork made of bits and pieces of colors*

Ms. Demeanor *Play on words for "misdemeanor," not behaving*

Muffin *An affectionate name*

Mystery *Secret, difficult to explain*

Mystique *Mystical feelings surrounding an individual*

Nadja *Short for Russian feminine name Nadjescha*

Nanna *Nickname for Anna*

Naomi *Hebrew origin, meaning "my delight"*

Natalie *Nickname for French name Natalia*

Naughty *Mischievous, not behaving properly*

Nelly *Combination of Helen and Eleanor*

Nightshade *Poisonous plant*

Nina *Endearment, Spanish for "daughter"*

Noche *Spanish for "evening"*

Noodles *Silly and fun*

Nora *Short for Leonora*

Norma *A constellation in the Milky Way*

Nutter Butter *A name of a nutty, buttery cookie*

Nymph *Nature goddess*

The Most Lovable Names for Cuddlers and Couch Potatoes

Mimi: always a true heartbreaker; Caro: from the Latin for "true friend"; Balu: after the lovable bear with savoir-vivre in the *Jungle Book*; Daddy: a dog daddy who goes about everything calmly; Mia: a tender, affectionate form of Maria; Mousy: cuddling included right in the name; Bunny: a dog that hops into your heart; Marshmallow: sweet and mushy like candy.

Olive *Variation on Olivia*
Olympia *Feminine Greek name for site of Olympic Games*
Opal *Precious stone that reflects light in various colors*
Ophelia *Greek for "helper," the woman in love with Hamlet in Shakespeare's play* Hamlet
Orchid *Distinctive, brightly colored tropical flower*
Ornament *Decoration or embellishment*

Paisley *An intricate pattern and design*
Paloma *Spanish for "dove"*
Pandora *In Greek mythology, the first mortal woman*
Pansy *A bright flower*
Paola *Italian for Paula*
Papillon *French for "butterfly"*
Paprika *A powdered red pepper, good for a reddish-colored and sassy dog*
Passion *Deep emotion, a brand of perfume*
Pastel *Light, soft color*
Patch *A patch of color, also Patches*

HIS MASTER'S VOICE

Many people still have not heard his name, but everyone knows his picture. For more than a hundred years the terrier mix has been sitting in front of the horn of a gramophone and listening to the music. Nipper lived from 1884 to 1895 in England. In 1900 the first magazine ads for the Gramophone Company with the Nipper theme appeared. Later the tagline "His Master's Voice" became the slogan. Today, Nipper is the trademark of the EMI record company.

Paula *Latin for "little one"*
Peaches *Endearment, sweet, loving*
Pearl *Precious rounded gem, ideal for black or white dog*
Pebbles *The baby daughter in the cartoon series* The Flintstones
Penelope *Faithful wife of Odysseus in Homer's* The Odyssey
Penny *A good-luck coin, nickname for Penelope*
Pepsi *Lively and energetic, a popular soft drink, for a dog with a bubbly personality*

Perdita *Heroine Dalmatian in Disney's* 101 Dalmatians
Petula *Feminine name, singer Petula Clark*
Petunia *Colorful garden flower*
Phoebe *Goddess of the moon in Greek mythology*
Piñata *A papier-mâché animal-shaped container filled with candy*
Pinta *Feminine name for "pinto," splotched colors*
Polaris *The North Star*
Polly *Short for English name Apollonia*
Porsche *Expensive German sports car*
Posh *Elegant and fashionable*
Precious *Beloved, dear, of great value*

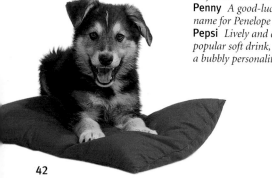

Princess *Royalty, the daughter of a queen*
Prudence *Feminine name from Latin, wise, discreet, careful*
Pumpkin *Term of endearment*

QT *As in "cutie"*
Queen *Royalty, also Queenie*

Rags *For the dog with messy hair*
Rainbow *Ideal for a colorful dog*
Raisin *A fun name for a small, sweet, dark dog. Variation Raison, as in* raison d'être *(French for "reason to be")*
Ramona *Feminine for Ramon*
Rapunzel *The girl with long, golden hair in Grimm's fairy tale "Rapunzel"*
Razzledazzle *Flashy, bewildering*
Razzmatazz *Lively excitement, also Razz*
Reba *Short for Rebecca, the captivator*
Rena *Short for Irene or Renata*
Renaissance *French for "rebirth," also Renny*
Renée *French for Renate, or "reborn"*
Revlon *A brand of cosmetics*
Rhonda *Beach Boys song "Help Me Rhonda"*
Rikki *Powerful ruler, feminine of Ricardo*
Risa *Short for Amarisa*
Rosey *Beautiful, fragrant flower, also Rosie, Rosa*
Roxanne *Cyrano's love in* Cyrano de Bergerac *by Rostand*
Ruby *Precious red gem*

Sabrina *Princess, teenage witch on the TV series* Sabrina the Teenage Witch
Sadie *A variation of Sarah*
Saffron *A very expensive, yellow spice, the perfect name for a yellowish dog*
Sahara *The world's largest desert, in North Africa*
Sally *A variation of Sarah*
Salsa *Latin American dance music, a hot dip*
Samantha *Feminine name for Samuel or Sam*
Sandy *Orphan Annie's dog, light brown color*
Sapphire *A blue gem*
Sarah *Meaning "royalty," "princess"*
Sasha *Helper, also Sascha or Sacha*
Sassy *Lively and spirited, the cat in the movie* The Incredible Journey
Savanne *French for "savannah," grasslands"*

Scarlett *Scarlett O'Hara, main character in Margaret Mitchell's book* Gone with the Wind, *play on words "Scarlet O'Hairy"*
Scribbles *For a dog with interesting coat patterns or markings*
Scully *FBI agent in the TV series* The X-Files
Señorita *Spanish for "miss"*
Serena *Tranquil, serene, variation Serina*
Shady Lady *A lady of secrecy and mystery*
Shana *Gift of grace*
Shannon *A river in Ireland*
Shasta *Sweet and bubbly, a mountain in California*
Sheba *Queen of Sheba, wealthy queen*
Sheila *Australian slang for "girl"*
Sherry *A dry wine*
Sienna *City in Italy, clay-earth color*

The Immortal Names from Painting and Music

Leonardo: the famed Italian artist; Madonna: a singing artist who knows no borders; Tosca: the diva from Puccini's opera; Satchmo: blues in the blood like Louis "Satchmo" Armstrong; Caruso: a star tenor who makes hearts melt; Figaro: loose and easy like *The Marriage of Figaro*; Elvis: rock around the clock.

Siren *In Greek mythology, a seductive sea nymph*
Smooch *Hug or kiss, lovable*
Smudge *Good for a dark dog or one with dark markings*
Snowy *Ideal for a white dog*
Soot *A black or dark dog*
Sophie *Skill, wisdom, variation of Sophia*
Sorbet *Colorful, sweet, icy dessert*
Star *Star of the show*
Stardust *Enchanting, dream-like, cluster of faraway stars*
Stella *Short for Estella, meaning "stellar, starlike"*
Sugar *Sweet, lovable*
Summer *For a dog born in the summertime*
Sweetie *Sweet, lovable, also Sweetie Pie*
Sweet Pea *A flower, term of endearment*
Sylvie *French for Sylvia*

Tabitha *Greek for "gazelle," a fast animal, also Tabby*
Taffy *A chewy, sweet candy*
Tammy *From the Russian name Tamara, also Tara*
Tanja *Short for Tatjana, also Tanya, Tonya*
Tasha *Short for Natasha*
Tequila *A Mexican alcoholic drink*
Tessa *Short for Theresa, meaning harvester, also Tess, Tessie*
Tiffany *Fancy New York jewelers, movie Breakfast at Tiffany's*
Tilly *Nickname for Emily or Matilda*
Tina *Short for Christina*

The Most Original Names of Famous Men and Women

Gandhi: a champion for peace; Oprah: Oprah Winfrey, talk show host; Marilyn: unforgettable Monroe; Florence: Florence Nightingale, the angel of the sick; Pavarotti: Luciano, the opera star of Italy and the world; Jesse: Jesse James, the outlaw of the wild west; Ringo: forever on the Beatles' drum set; Hitch: affectionate for the master of mystery, Alfred Hitchcock.

Tinkerbell *The tiny fairy in James Barrie's story* Peter Pan
Tiny *A name for a very, very small dog*
Tori *Short for Victoria*
Tosca *Main character in Puccini's opera* Tosca
Tracy *English name short for Theresa, also Tracie*
Trixie *Clever, lucky*
Truffles *For a sweet, chocolate-colored dog*
Tweety *The little canary in Warner Brothers animated cartoons, first named Tweetie Pie*
Twiggy *Super-thin model, good for a slender breed dog*

Una *Latin for unity, number one*
Ursula *Latin for she-bear, legendary British princess*
Ute *German feminine name, also Uta*

Valerie *Feminine name of Latin origin, also Val*
Vanessa *Actress Vanessa Redgrave*
Vanilla *Name for a white dog, fragrant plant used in flavoring*
Venus *Goddess of love and beauty in Roman mythology*
Victoria *Victory, feminine for Victor*
Violet *A plant with bright flowers, also Viola or Vi*
Vivian *The enchantress and mistress of Merlin the magician in the King Arthur legends, French for "lively"*

Wags *Barbie doll's toy dog Tag Along Wags*
Waif *Name for a small or thin dog, variation Wafer, as in "cookie"*
Wampum *String of beads made of shells used by Native*

Americans for ornaments and money
Wanda *The wanderer*
Wendy *A variation of Wanda*
Whitney *Singer Whitney Houston, mountain in California*
Wiggles *A very active, wiggly dog*
Wilma *English name, short for Wilhelmina, Fred Flintstone's wife in the animated cartoon series* The Flintstones
Winnie *Winnie the Pooh, bear in story by A. A. Milne*

Xandra *Variation of Alexandra*
Xaveria *Unique, exotic feminine name*
Xena *Variation on Xenia, also Zena*
Xenia *Greek meaning "hospitable to strangers"*
Xuxa *Fun, unusual name*

Yakira *Hebrew for "expensive"*
Yappy *A talkative dog, also Yappie*
Yara *Brazilian name thought to be derived from "January"*
Yvette *French name, original meaning "oak tree," "acorn"*

Zara *Prosperous*
Zenzi *Short for Innozentia*
Zinfandel *A red wine from California*
Zerlinda *Calm, beautiful*
Zigzag *Design, path, also Ziggy*
Zodiac *Path of the planets, moon, and sun*
Zoey *Meaning "life"*

DOGS AND THEIR PEOPLE

Millie: English springer spaniel belonging to ex-president George Bush; Muggsie: Marilyn Monroe's collie; Buddy: the Labrador of ex-president Bill Clinton; Martha: Paul McCartney's German shepherd; Blackie: Hemingway's companion; Poor Pooh: Prince Charles's Jack Russell; Charley: John Steinbeck's poodle; Lucy: Jodie Foster's boxer; Fala: Franklin D. Roosevelt's terrier

INDEX

A Adventurers, Pirates and 8
Astrology   15

B Baby Boomer and Mommy's Sweetheart 9
Bad Behavior   17
Breeding Dogs   14

C Character Types   8, 9
Choosing a Name   5, 6, 7, 10, 11
Couch Potatoes, Cuddlers and   9
Curiosity of a Young Dog 12

D Dog Breeds   14
Dog Horoscope   15
Dog Stories   23, 28, 30, 35, 38, 42
Dog Training   12, 13
Dogs, Unforgettable   21

F Famous Dogs   21
Fashionable Names   10
Female Dogs, Names for 33–45
   Top Ten Names for   37

H Horoscope for Dogs   15

K Kennel Names   6, 14

L Learning a Name   6, 16, 17

M Macho and Maestro   8
Male Dogs, Top Ten Names for   26
Moody and Sleeping Beauty   9
Mommy's Sweetheart, Baby Boomer and   9

N Name, Choosing a   5, 6, 7, 10, 11
Names
   Famous   21
   from A to Z   20–45
   for Baby Boomers and Mommy's Sweetheart 36
   for Couples and Partners 33
   for Cuddlers and Couch Potatoes   41
   for Female Dogs 33–45
   for Friends and Chums 32
   for Machos and Maestros   31
   for Male Dogs   20–32
   for Pirates and Adventurers   25
   for Princes and Princesses   22
   for Shy Dogs and Sleeping Beauties   39
   for Smart Dogs   40
   from Comics and Cartoons   29
   from Fairy Tales and Fables   27
   from Movies and Television   24
   from Painting and Music   43
   from Sagas   34
   from World Literature 20
   of Famous Men and Women   44
Name Training   11, 16, 17
Nicknames   6

P Pirates and Adventurers 8
Positive Reinforcement 13
Puppy School   12, 13
Puppy Training   12, 13
Purebred Dogs   14

S Signs of the Zodiac   15
Sleeping Beauty, Moody and   9
Socialization for Puppies 13
Stars and Dog Names   45
Stories About Dogs   23, 28, 30, 35, 38, 42

T Taboo Names   7
Top Ten Names for Female Dogs   37
Top Ten Names for Male Dogs   26
Training   12, 13
Trendy Names   7, 10

ADRESSES

Dog Organizations
➤ American Kennel Club
5580 Centerview Drive,
Suite 200
Raleigh, NC 27606-3390
(919) 233-9780

➤ American Rare Breeds
Association
9921 Frank Tippett Road
Cheltenham, MD 20673
(301) 868-5718

➤ Canadian Kennel Club
100-89 Skyway Avenue
Etobicoke, Ontario
M9W6R4 Canada
(416) 675-5511

➤ Fédération Cynologique
Internationale (FCI)
Place Albert 1er 13
B-6530 Thuin, Belgium
www.fci.be

➤ National Bird Dog
Museum
505 West Highway 57
P.O. Box 744
Grand Junction, TN 88039
(901) 764-2058

➤ United Kennel Club
100 East Kilgore Road
Kalamazoo, MI 49002-5584
(616) 434-9020

Dogs on the Internet
➤ Dog breeds in alphabetical
order: *www.dogbreedinfo.
com/abc.htm*

➤ PetCare dog breed infor-
mation: *www.petcare.umn.
edu/Dogs/Breed.htm*

➤ List of Dog Breeds:
*www.akc.org/breeds/
recbreeds/breeds_a.cfm*

➤ AKC glossary: *www.akc.
org/love/glossary.cfm*

➤ FCI dog breeds: *www.fci.
be/nomenclatures*

Questions About Dog Ownership
You can get addresses of dog
clubs and associations from
the foregoing associations
and Internet contacts. Pet
shop professionals and
Humane Society personnel
can answer your questions
about dog ownership.

Liability and Health Insurance
Check with your preferred
insurance company or
agency; some companies
offer liability insurance for
dog owners and health
insurance for their dogs.

Dog Registry
You can protect your dog
from animal thieves and
loss by entering it into a
dog registry. Entry and
computer-assisted search
upon report of a missing
dog are free.

Helpful Books
➤ American Kennel Club.
The Complete Dog Book.
New York, NY: Howell Book
House, 1992.
➤ Ammen, Amy. *Training
in No Time: An Expert's
Approach to Effective Dog
Training for Hectic Life
Styles.* New York, NY:
Howell Book House, 1995.
➤ Bailey, Gwen. *The Well
Behaved Dog.* Hauppauge,
NY: Barron's Educational
Series, Inc., 1998.
➤ Davis, Kathy Diamond.
Responsible Dog Ownership.
New York, NY: Howell Book
House, 1994.
➤ Ludwig, Gerd. *Sit! Stay!
Train Your Dog the Easy
Way.* Hauppauge, NY:
Barron's Educational Series,
Inc., 1998.
➤ Rice, Dan. *The Dog
Handbook.* Hauppauge, NY:
Barron's Educational Series,
Inc., 1999.

➤ Smith, Cheryl S. *Pudgy Pooch, Picky Pooch.* Hauppauge, NY: Barron's Educational Series, Inc., 1998.
➤ Taunton, Stephanie J. and Cheryl S. Smithy. *The Trick Is in the Training.* Hauppauge, NY: Barron's Educational Series, Inc., 1998.

Periodicals
➤ *AKC Gazette*
Subscriptions: (919) 233-9767

➤ *Dog Fancy*
P. O. Box 53264
Boulder, CO 80322

➤ *Dog World*
29 North Wacker Drive
Chicago, IL 60606

➤ *Off-Lead*
204 Lewis Street
Canastota, NY 13032
(800) 241-7619

THE AUTHOR

Zoologist and author Dr. Gerd Ludwig was editor in chief of the monthly magazine *Das Tier.* Today he works as a freelance journalist, book author, media reporter, and seminar leader. He has written several how-to books on dog and cat ownership, principally for the Graefe and Unzer Publishing Company.

Sharon Vanderlip, D.V.M., has written books and published articles in scientific and general interest publications. Dr. Vanderlip served as the Associate Director of Veterinary Services for the University of California at San Diego School of Medicine, and is the recipient of various awards for her writing and dedication to animal health.

THE PHOTOGRAPHERS

Bilder Pur/Hermeline/Cogis: page 8 left; Juniors: page 9 right; Juniors/Botzenhard: page 9 left; Juniors/Schanz: page C2, 3 bottom, C4 left; Juniors/Steimer: page C1, 7, 8 middle; Juniors/Wegler: page 11, 18, C4, right; Steimer: page 2 top, 3 top right, 9 middle, 16, 21, 26, 32, 38, 42, C4 top; Wegler: page 2 bottom, 3 left, 4, 8 right, 13, 14, 17, 23, 25, 29, 30, 35, 37, 41, 45.

TRANSLATOR

Eric A. Bye, M.A., is a lifelong dog owner and a translator from French, Spanish, and German who lives and works in Vermont.

First edition for the United States, its territories and dependencies and Canada published in 2005 by Barron's Educational Series, Inc.

All inquiries should be addressed to:
Barron's Educational Series, Inc.
250 Wireless Boulevard
Hauppauge, NY 11788
www.barronseduc.com

ISBN-13: 978-0-7641-3071-7
ISBN-10: 0-7641-3071-4

Library of Congress Catalog Card No. 2004114878

Printed and bound in China
9 8 7 6 5 4